# Data Analytics & Business Intelligence

SADANAND PUJARI

Published by SADANAND PUJARI, 2023.

# Table of Contents

# Copyright

**Data Analytics & Business Intelligence**

First Edition: Dec 2023

Book Design by **SADANAND PUJARI**

# About

If you wish to make a successful career in this super trending area of data analytics and business intelligence commanding huge pay packages, then this is perfectly the right Book for you to get you started. Besides going into detail of understanding data and performing meaningful analytics on it, this Business Intelligence & Data Analytics Book also introduces you briefly to the concepts of machine learning and data science.

Data gathering, storage, and knowledge management are combined with data analysis in business intelligence systems to evaluate and transform complex data into meaningful, actionable information that can be used to support more effective strategic, tactical, and operational insights and decision-making. An organization's business intelligence environments are made up of a number of technologies, applications, processes, strategies, products, and technological architectures that are used to gather, analyze, display, and disseminate internal and external business data.

The use of methodologies such as data mining, predictive analytics, and statistical analysis in order to analyze and transform data into useful information, identify and anticipate trends and outcomes, and ultimately make smarter, data-driven business decisions, is referred to as business intelligence and analytics, a data management solution and business intelligence subset.

A business intelligence platform allows companies to take use of their current data architecture and construct unique business intelligence apps that allow analysts to query and view data. Self-service analytics is supported by modern business intelligence solutions, making it simple for end users to build their own reports. Users may connect to a variety of data sources, including NoSQL databases, Hadoop systems, cloud platforms, and traditional data warehouses, using simple user interfaces mixed with flexible business intelligence backend software to produce a unified picture of their heterogeneous data.

This Business Intelligence and Data Analytics Book aims to produce a select group of skilled individuals who are cross-trained in business process analysis, technology management, and technically skilled in all aspects of data science, such as predictive modeling, analytical reporting, GIS mapping, segmentation analysis, and data visualization along with machine learning & deep learning. Students will acquire the skills to integrate cutting edge information and analytics technologies with best practices and applied business methods.

The Business Intelligence & Analytics Book combines analytical and professional skills to help you become the type of manager who questions assumptions and makes evidence-based choices based on facts. You'll learn new skills that will help you improve your goods, services, and strategies while leading your firm through markets that are always changing due to technological advancements. Machine learning, language processing, data mining, data modeling including predictive modeling, optimization, NoSQL, NLP are among the topics covered in the curriculum, which are at the forefront of the data revolution.

Classes go beyond the fundamentals of understanding data and using it for making business decisions, to addressing essential business ideas.

# Introduction to the Book

Hi again. I am very happy to see you here. Your time is your most valuable asset. That is why I'm very grateful that you have chosen to spend some time with me in this Book. I hope that you would have an exciting journey through the world of data and analytics because this is an analytics training. I wanted to put some facts to stress how important it is for everyone today to know about it. More than 46 percent of businesses use business intelligence tools as a core element of their strategy.

Together with analytics tools, business intelligence software is projected to reach twenty six billion by the end of this year. But despite these facts, a Gartner study says that 87 percent of organizations have low BI and analytics maturity. That means that there are plenty of opportunities out there to improve and for you to grow your career. By the end of 2020, the number of job profiles that require analytics knowledge will increase from 300,000 to almost three million openings. Only in the United States, there is currently a shortage of 190,000 people with analytical skills. Now allow me to provide some background from the Book.

I will define this as a crash Book. We would cover many matters and principles around data that would bring you up to speed to the conversations that happen in most companies around the world today. But even more important, you will learn how to apply analytics and critical thinking to your job because this training will focus on business analytics. The art of analyzing data to make money. The techniques that we will cover will serve you either if you work for a large company in a startup or if you're a blogger. They are agnostic to the type of business because every single organization, even the smallest one, generates data and you can use this data to improve results.

My aim is that at the end of this Book, you have a data driven mindset so that when you attend your next meeting or interview you can ask the right questions. I have also seen users very excited to specialize in one or multiple of the matters after this training. I remember a person becoming a reference for business intelligence in her company after a training session. She found her real passion in analytics. The Book has several chapters or chapters being the three main descriptive, predictive and prescriptive analytics.

Data Management as an enabler of these three and Data Life cycle Which is more general domain knowledge. There will be some homework as you will be appointed the CEO of a Hotel company during the training and you will need to use data to make some important decisions. You will also go through knowledge tests after the most important chapters.

This Book is not about coding or learning a specific analytics tool. There are many of these around. However, we will touch upon some of the most popular programming languages and analytics instruments. Finally, I sincerely hope that the chapters on materials sharing this Book can be applied effectively in your career with these few remarks. I thank you for listening to me and declaring the Books officially open. May you have a productive and successful training.

# Definition of Analytics

Welcome back to the very first chapter of these data analytics ultimate Book for beginners in this chapter. We're going to speak about some definitions of what is analytics as well as the history and some of these buzzwords that you're hearing every day, everywhere. Let us start with a definition of analytics. So what is actually analytics? If we look at Wikipedia, analytics is defined as the discovery, interpretation and communication of meaningful patterns in data. Indeed, there are two important chapters in this definition of analytics by Wikipedia.

The first one is the discovery and interpretation. And this is gonna be a constant across these Books. We need to find patterns and do the interpretation of it. The second one is communication. And this is super important. And we will speak a lot about this because it's very important that all the facts, findings that we search through data are properly communicated. Analytics is a vast domain. And it keeps growing every day. It involves activities like acquiring, transforming and storing data.

Applying domain knowledge, reporting results or more advanced forecasting. And Predictive algorithms When we talk about Analytics. It's important to differentiate the two flavors. The first one is non-business analytics. When we talk about non-business analytics, we speak, for example, about government studies like the GDP, public health, academic research or explorative analytics like astrology, an example of non-business analytics. It's where we're suffering today with the Covid 19. If you look at the dashboard, you can see how the pandemy of the corona viruses is spreading around the world. But it doesn't have a business outcome.

It can have interpretations for business, obviously. But it's not built for business. The second flavor of an Analytics and the one that is the core of this Book is business analytics and business analytics is defined as the application of technologies and practices to improve business performance decisions and plan. This is using data to improve the way we do business. Let's see an example, a hotel chain has been capturing reservations, but that has been made in a few last years. But when they receive the data all they can see is a spreadsheet with a hundred twenty thousand records. That's not very useful.

Let's now see how analytics have helped transform all this information into more actionable insights. Look at the report we have on the screen. It's using exactly the same data that was seen in the spreadsheet. Now, this looks much better, right? Building a report like this from a hundred and twenty thousand records takes less than one hour. And this is where data analytics is all about simplifying information, finding patterns and communicating them, I guess. Now you understand why analytics is so important nowadays.

Data is the biggest asset of this century and the ability to capture, read and understand it. We give businesses big and small a tremendous competitive advantage. But analytics is more than a hard skill. Analytics is more like a few lines of coding or just putting together a dashboard or a beautiful visual Analytics is an art. Analytics requires design knowledge because the data has to be visualized. You need to play with colors, space and user interfaces. It also requires domain knowledge to be able to apply findings to real business problems.

Finally, it requires writing skills to be able to summarize hundreds and thousands of records in just one headline. A few takeaways from this chapter. Analytics is about finding patterns in data. This Book is focusing on business analytics. Lastly, analytics is a huge bucket with many disciplines in sight. And it keeps growing. In the next chapter, we will have a look at the history of Analytics.

# History of Analytics

Welcome back. In chapter number two, we're going to speak about the history of Analytics, where does analytics come from. If we look at the etymology of the word, it seems that the word analytical and the related verb analyze, comes from ancient Greek. More precisely from the verb. analysis Which means to break up or to loosen. But despite being more than 2000 years old. Meaning has prevailed. Today we say that is Analytica. If you are good at taking a problem, breaking it down into smaller elements and solving it, let's have a look at the evolution of politics and history.

During ancient Egypt, we'd find the first new medical operations. And later on with Mesopotamians, left a trace of using these numerical operations for analytics. Now we take a big leap and we go to the 70s. And this is where relational databases were invented. And also the very things SQL language. These databases provided the advantage of being able to analyze data on demands. In the 80s and due to the increase of data and the necessity of storing it, we saw the birth of the first data warehouses.

The term business intelligence was first used in 1865, but Howard Dresner at Gartner in 1989 would describe it as making better business decisions through searching, gathering and analyzing the accumulated data saved by an organization. Right after. In the 90s. Again, data mining and in 1996, for the very first time, the term data science was used in your conference in Kobe, Japan. In 2005, we saw the birth of their very famous term 'Big Data' Roger Magoulas described large amounts of data as Big Data. A few takeaways on this chapter, Analytics is thousands of years old. But is it still about breaking down big problems? And in the last 50 years, it boomed, driven by the beginning of the digital age. In 2002, the increase of storing and computing capacity.

# Analytics Buzzwords

Welcome back to chapter three, 'Buzz Words'. In this chapter, we will talk about some of the most heard terms in the world of data and analytics. We will explain them and demystify some of them. Some others will be covered in detail in future chapters. We will start by talking about the probably most famous terms in the world of data and analytics, big data. This gentleman is called Roger Mougalas. And in 2005, he coined the term Big Data. Roger was working with a large data set. That was almost impossible to manage. And because he didn't have the tools.

To manage this data set back at a time he invented the term big data. But big data has evolved. And nowadays we talk about big data. When we speak about complex data sets that come from one or many sources that require And here's the important part. Advanced techniques and software in order to analyze it. Therefore, big data does not always mean large data sets. And you can have a spreadsheet and a big database. And both of them. Could be defined as big data. A.I. Artificial Intelligence. It's computers mimicking human processes and decision making abilities. It takes information and context and provides advice or solutions.

The context part is super important because it's what makes A.I. so powerful. I can blend the weather with the probability of buying an umbrella. AI is giving computers the ability to think. ML ML or machine learning. Is a subset of artificial intelligence and it consists in giving systems the ability to learn without being explicitly programmed. Have a look at the right hand side. We have a very simple algorithmic operation there. One plus one equals two. We as humans are able to deduct that if one plus one is two, one plus two would be three. Traditionally, computers were programmed. To compute one plus two. But nowadays, with machine learning, computers can learn. And deduct that one plus two will be three without the need of giving explicit instruction. Another example of machine learning is your social media feeds your Facebook that continuously suggests you new things, new pages, new friends to follow or to invite all these are algorithm using machine learning Augmented analytics, augmented analytics is no other thing than technologies such as machine learning and AI That help assist with data preparation, inside generation and insights.

Usually all these tasks are performed by data scientists who spend 80 percent of their time collecting and preparing data. The goal of augmented analytics is to automate all of these processes so that data scientists will spend 20 percent of the time preparing the data and 80 percent of the time driving insights. Seltzer is B.A.. It enables business users to access and work with data, even if they don't have a background in statistical analysis, math or business intelligence. It's literally the concept of a supermarket with an aisle and you go on big data that you need. It has become very popular in the last year, thanks to tools like Tableau or Power BI That make it very easy, putting together visualization, data visualization by dragging and dropping items. NLP or natural language processing, it's processing text in order to classify cluster search or extract information. NLP is all about text.

The algorithms will read and interpret a great amount of text and create taxonomies and categories or apply sentiment analysis. Think about your email anti spam filter when your email provider classifies an email as spam. It's probably reading the entire context or the content of the e-mail and the subject and determining through algorithms that this is probably spam. Mobile analytics. It's a very easy one. It's enabled business users to access a lot of data through their mobile devices so that they can make decisions on the spot. Hadoop. Hadoop is a set of open source programs. That means that anyone can use and modify them. This is also why it has become very popular.

Hadoop harnesses the power of distributed computing and distributed storage. Hadoop can run multiple processes in parallel, using different computers and sets of computers to handle very, very, very large amounts of data using batch processing. Hadoop is the preferred big data to go tool Because it provides very good performance and the costs are low. Unstructured versus unstructured data. Think about structured data as data that is logically formatted and usually in the form of a spreadsheet or a tabular format or a table. Unstructured data has some structure, but is not structured via predefined data models of schema. Doesn't have a predefined structure. Think about unstructured data. When you read an email, there is logic in an email. It's logically written. But the data is not structuring a predefined format. Data Lake. Data Lake is a system of data stored in its natural raw format, usually in the form of files.

Think about a data lake as an external hard drive or your cloud drive where you put every kind of file. Could be CSV, text files, It could be music. Could be a song. Could be a PDF. So this is exactly what a Data Lake is. Then after there are several processes and Hadoop is usually one of them involved that will cluster, classify all this information to make it readable. Insights. I would like to finish this chapter explaining the difference between data, information and insights. Data is the raw and unprocessed facts that we capture. Data, It's the information that we get in remember chapter one? We spoke about the hotel reservations in a spreadsheet. This is data. Information is when this data has been processed. And we use it to understand something, usually a problem. And insights are gained when you analyze these data. And you make solutions for a particular situation.

Usually this comes in the form of decisions. If you look at the chart in this is the funnel of data, information and insights. We collect the raw facts. We structure and format them. Finally, we bring insights to take action. Let's make a quick recap on chapter one of the Book. First of all, the definition of analytics, identifying patterns in the data and communicating them. Second, the history of analytics. It started thousands of years ago. That is in the last 50 years with the digital era when it has boomed. Last but not least, I will pick only one buzz word to define, Big Data. Big Data is not large data sets or a lot of data. Big Data is a complex data that requires special techniques to be analyzed. See you in the next chapter.

# Analytics Landscape: Descriptive, Predictive, Prescriptive

Hi and welcome to chapter number two. In this model, with only one chapter, you will get to know the three main groups of analytics: descriptive, predictive and prescriptive. These three and englobe, almost all modern analytic methods, compliment each other and in many cases, one can enable others. By the end of this chapter, you will clearly understand how the different analytics types split into past, present and future.

From now onward, you will be the CEO of the hotel chain of the first chapter. Congratulations. But that means that you will need to make decisions based on what the data will tell you. So keep your eyes and ears very open. You can find the hotel data set and the other resources in the Book materials. Let us start. Descriptive Analytics. What happened? Descriptive analytics is the base of analytics. It's the foundation, the eldest and what most businesses do today. Descriptive analytics takes data and turns it into digestible chunks. Some of the questions it can answer are what happened, why it happened or when it happened.

Going back to the hotel example, some questions could be. Which hotel made more money in the last three years? Which channel is contributing to more reservations? The methods used are data aggregation, dashboards, reports and traditional data analysis. Some of the most popular tools are Excel Power BI, Tableau, Qlik or Business Objects and Cognos. Your hotel chain has two hotels, one in the city and a resort on the beach. So you might be wondering what has happened in the last few years with your properties. Let's take a look back and see what happened, and we can see that the city hotel contributed 70 percent of the revenue. And why? It's because tribal agents are much more likely to book the city hotel than the resort hotel. Descriptive analytics looks into the past to help you understand what has happened. It answers questions like how much money your business has made or what are your best selling products.

This is what 90 percent of companies are doing today. It also serves as a foundation for the other two prescriptive and predictive. I will give you a piece of voluntary homework today. What other questions would you like to ask descriptive analytics about the performance of your hotel? Predictive analytics. What will happen? Predictive analytics is about previewing the future. It provides estimates about the likelihood of something to happen. It is important to remember that there is no statistical algorithm that can predict the future with 100 percent of certainty.

Predictive analytics answers questions like what will happen or when will it happen? How many reservations will we get next year? What is the probability for a customer to come back to your property? Some popular methods for predictive analytics are forecasting risk modeling, customer segmentation and sentiment analysis. Tools like R programming language, Database Visualization and other tools like SPSS, Python or Apache Spark are among the most used for predictive analytics. Let's go back to your hotel chain. Would you be able to make better proactive decisions if you know what might happen next year? Probably, yes. How can predictive analytics tell you what is going to happen with your hotels?

In this example and inside the Red Square, we can see the forecast of what can happen in the future. It seems that you will have a drop of revenue in the summer of 2017, which will recover starting the year after. If you know this information in advance, it's very likely that you can take decisions to help recover the dips. Predictive analytics allows us to fast forward into the future. How much might we sell next year or will customers come back? Now that you have seen what the future is for your hotels. Tell us what actions you think you should take. Prescriptive analytics. What should you do? Prescriptive analytics.

Provides recommendations of different possible actions to optimize your business outcomes. It is the most optimized as well, most complex form of analytics because it deals with so many variables. Some questions like what should I do or how can I make it happen? And uses like what should be the price of my products. What should be the price of my rooms next summer? Methodology is like machine learning. Algorithms and data modeling are often used for prescriptive analytics and tools like Alteryx, Python, Rapidminer or Sisense are among the most famous. So what if analytics could tell you what is the ideal price for your hotel room? That'll be great. In fact, using models and algorithms, we can see that in August you should be applying the highest price to your hotel rooms. Not only that, if we look at the overbooking rates, those rooms that you can over sell, because you know that there will be some cancellations.

July provides you with the month with the highest cancellation rate and therefore you can oversell your rooms more. But in December, your customers are less likely to cancel. Prescriptive analytics is pretty much about recommendations to make things happen. What should be my next product? What price should I market? Now, if you could ask your analytics department one question, what should you do with your hotel strategy? What will it be? I would like to introduce you to the analytics value escalator created by Gartner. It's a simple chart that illustrates very well the journey that many businesses follow through data analytics. If you can see at the very beginning, bottom left, we have descriptive analytics. This is the base where, where we start as we move to the The difficulty increases, but also the value. Then we go to what will happen, predictive analytics to end up with the most complex form of analytics that is prescriptive analytics. How can we make things happen?

The most powerful, but also the most complex. A summary of this chapter, descriptive it's looking in the past at what happened when it happened. Uses data aggregation and dashboards and tools like Excel or Tableau. Predictiveness is the future. What will happen? Forecasting, customer segmentation and tools like R or statistical software like SPSS? Finally prescriptive, what should you do? It's the most complex form with machine learning.

Algorithms and tools like Alteryx, Python or Rapid Miner. A summary of chapter 2, Descriptive is what happened in the past. Is the base and it's what most companies are doing today. Prediction tells us what is going to happen in the future? And prescriptive. The most advanced form of analytics. Tell us what to do to get the best business out. In the next chapter, we will see descriptive analytics and its methodologies.

# Business Intelligence

Welcome to the chapter Descriptive Analytics. In the following chapters You will know the analytics techniques that are used by most companies as well as how to apply them. In this chapter, we will speak about BI or Business Intelligence. I'd like to start this chapter with a quote from one of my favorite characters. I never guess. It is a capital mistake to theorize before one has data, insensibly one begins to twist facts, to sweep theories instead of theories to suit facts. As you might have guessed. This was written by Arthur Conan Doyle, the creator of Sherlock Holmes. And I think it's summarized perfectly why we always need to look at data and why are you here. Let's look at the definition of what Business Intelligence is.

Business intelligence refers to the applications, infrastructure, tools and best practices that enable us to access and analyze information to improve and optimize decisions on performance. The components of BI: Applications usually come in the form of dashboards and reports, infrastructure, data warehousing. Also data sets, tools like sequel programming languages. We will see later on, Power BI, Tableau or Qlik and best practices is Data Quality. And we will see data quality in almost every chapter of this chapter. In the next video created by the company Hitachi. You will have a great summary of what Business Intelligence is.

You may have heard the term Business Intelligence or B.I. But what does that really mean? There are several different definitions. But to put it simply, B.I is about delivering relevant and reliable information to the right people at the right time with the goal of achieving better decisions faster. To do this, B.I requires methods and programs to collect unstructured data converted into information and present it to improve business decisions. B.I. takes the vast amount of data generated by businesses and presents it in a meaningful, actionable way. Well, these are simple concepts. B.I is actually a large and complex field, including performance management, analytics, predictive modeling, data and text mining and a lot more. Imagine business intelligence functioning like a grocery store when you enter a grocery store and are looking for specific items, say eggs, milk and bananas.

You do not need to find an employee to ask them where to look. Instead, grocery stores are organized into aisles and signs that make the store relatively simple to navigate. Now imagine the items in the store are like your business's data, and you need to collect information on production, billable hours and sales goals. You are likely to go to three different experts and ask them where you can find this information. Then you will go to someone else and have them compile it for you. B.I is all about taking your messy information and turning it into a tidy and accessible grocery store. This enables you to navigate your data on your own and find what you need without relying on others. Organizations no longer have to dig through complex webs of links, spreadsheets, analyzing the data manually and mashing together reports instead. Employees can use B.I systems to request the information.

Using B.I offers significant advantages when trying to make strategic decisions. Having anytime access to organized data means that you can discover inefficient business processes and hidden patterns. Identify areas of strength and weakness and discover new opportunities, all of which contribute to a better understanding of your company's operations and challenges. Let's look at a retail example. You are the manager of a retail chain that has both stores and online shops. You offer your customers a loyalty card which they can swipe in the stores or enter into their online account. The card associates everything the customer buys in-store and online with their unique account number into your organization's databases through the use of business intelligence methods and software. You are empowered by having the ability to run analytical reports on massive amounts of customer information, which can enable you to understand how loyal they are to your brand.

What products they buy and how frequently. And if they have a preference for visiting the store or buying from the online store. What does this give you? The ability to understand or even predict an individual customer or segment needs preferences and habits, anticipate new opportunities to sell, deliver better service, or even provide targeted marketing campaigns such as instant delivery of coupons at point of sale for products related to their interests. As indicated by passive behavior. In short, you are able to understand your customers very well based on their historical transactions and behavior and use that information to increase your sales or differentiate your brand by providing better or unique services. So in closing, the term business intelligence refers to a group of tools and techniques that collects and organizes your data and presents it in a way that is useful and makes sense.

If you want to have efficient access to accurate, understandable and actionable information on demand, that business intelligence might be right for your organization. Let's have a look at some examples of what to do with B.I. Amazon uses B.I. to anticipate shoppers' purchases and cut down shipping time, how do they do it? Amazon studies your behaviors, and they may know beforehand that you usually order a certain product. That way they anticipate Shipping's and they might ship something to you or send it close to your location even before you have placed an order. B.I. can also help improve operational efficiency Heathrow Airport in London, which accounts for more than 80 million passengers every year, collects data from flight delays, weather or cargo.

And if, for example, the landing of 20 or 30 flights with 6,000 extra passengers is delayed They inform an application and alert immigration, customs and baggage handling so they can prepare the stuff that they need to handle the influx of passengers. Gartner, It's a global research advisory firm. We're gonna mention it a lot in this Book because it's an institution for B.I. and data analytics. Every year, Gartner releases the top tools in the magic quadrant, which comprises readiness, ambition of each tool. In the top right square, You can see the leaders and visionaries for B.I. Microsoft Power B.I. is leading at the moment, followed by Tableau and Qlik. Tableau was recently acquired by the sales for a group. It is the pioneer of drag and drop visualization and it has the largest community among all the B.I. tools.

Power B.I. The current leader for Gartner is part of Microsoft. It is a component of a suite of tools called power platform, and it has become very successful. After the integration with other office products. Qlik, the Swedish independent company, offered an end to end platform, which included data integration, user driven business intelligence and conversational analytics. Of course, there are many more tools used in the B.I. landscape, but these three are the most important at the moment. Self-service B.I. Its end users design and deploy their own reports and analysis within an approved and supported architecture and tools portfolio.

Let's see a quick demo on how self-service B.I. works. To illustrate the concept of self-service B.I. We will have a look at a dashboard that we have built using Power B.I. using the data of your hotel. As you can see, the self-service B.I. a feature from a dashboard helps you filter by any of the metrics that you have on screen. So you can see what's the performance of individual countries by date or by distribution channel. The second form of self-service B.I. More advanced is the DIY part (Do It Yourself). Using visualizations and the fields, the data points that are part of your datasets. You can easily build a chart that will show you the average rate of your rooms by years. So imagine how powerful this is in just a couple of clicks. Any end user with no technical knowledge can put together the information that they need to make decisions. Business Intelligence applied to your hotel chain.

Business Intelligence can tell us What and we already saw That your city hotel brings more revenue than your resort. When we can see that 27 things so far are the best year, but we grow less. Compared to 2015. Your hotel is mainly a property for adults with only five percent of children visiting your properties and

83% of your visitors choose Bed and breakfast as their meal option. A summary of Business Intelligence. B.I. is a combination of applications, infrastructure, tools and best practices.

The main output of B.I. is reports and dashboards. Self-service B.I. enables end users, technical or not, to consume and build reports. Business Intelligence takes care of a lot of data And transforms it back into digestible reports. and dashboards. B.I. is a foundational part of the data structure of every company. In the next chapter, Data analysis.

# Data analysis

In this chapter, you will learn about data analysis. Data analysis is a broad term and almost everything in this Book can be treated as data analysis. We will narrow it down to the general analysis made for business decisions. What is data analysis? It is the process of inspecting, cleansing, transforming a modeling data with the end goal of discovering useful information and super important supporting decision making. The different components are applications like presentations, reports or results. It uses infrastructure like data warehouses or several data sets. Tools like Excel, PowerPoint or PDF. And within the best practices.

We have data quality and insights generation. There are two types of data analysis. Quantitative, focuses on WHAT it is the process of collecting and evaluating measurable data such as revenues or market share to understand business behavior, it usually comes in terms of numerical values. The second type is qualitative analysis, which focuses on WHY. Why do people behave in certain ways or why do they not buy or not buy your product? It measures feelings, thoughts or perceptions to understand motivations and behaviors.

Data analysis for businesses is very often presented as a presentation that contains charts, captions and insights explaining the findings of one or more multiple data points. Going back to the example of your hotel, we have a takeaway. That is that sales are below our target, our expected sales, which is usually supported also by KPI key performance indicators. We also have insights like that Portugal accounts for most Almost half the revenue or that the segment that is declining is offline reservations, which has been overtaken by online sales. And this is supported by charts and background information or contextual information.

In summary, most of the analytics methodologies used today can be labeled as data analysis. Business Analysis are usually presentations combining multiple data sources and data points to provide insights and recommendations. As you have seen, data analysis is more than just one thing. Most of the analysis uses one or more analytics methodologies. But the important takeaway is that in today's business environment it usually serves as presentations that combine data, information and insights for better business decisions.

Data analysis is the bread and butter of analytics. Hundreds of presentations with insights are circulated every day across companies, and they help make informed decisions to the leaders. In the next chapter, market research.

# Market Research

Market research started in the 1920s during the golden age of radio. Companies that advertised on the radio wanted to understand the demographics to serve better ads. Since then, it has become a key pillar of qualitative information for companies. What is market research? Marketing research is any set of techniques used to gather information and better understand a company's target market. And here's the main difference between market research and other disciplines of analytics is about your target market.

Businesses will use the information to design better products, improve the user experience and craft a marketing message that is targeted and attracts quality leads and improve conversion rates. Components usually market research, applied to defined personas, identify cohorts or understand what's the potential of a product, a new product or an existing product. Market research uses qualitative datasets and the main tools are questionnaires, surveys, interviews and focus groups.

Best practices, customer journey mappings and affinity diagrams, look alike audiences etc.. There are two types of data for market research. The first one is primary information. This is information that we have gathered around our consumers, our customers, and it's first hand research. We collected through surveys or focus group discussions. The second set of data is called Secondary Information. It's collected in the past by someone else. For example, research on the Internet, newspaper articles, government publications, health care papers. All of these are secondary information.

Apply to your hotels and in the search for answers. We saw previously that your research is not growing on sales and is underperforming compared to your city hotel. So how could market research help us improve performance for the resort? Have a look at this small survey with just three questions. This is just an example with three questions targeted to hotel customers. Where will you usefully go on holiday? This will let us understand what is your segment if it's local, regional, national or international. Select the amenities that would be available in your ideal hotel. This tells us more about what your guests might be looking for.

Finally, which of the following hotel chains, if any, have you stayed in the past 12 months? We have some famous popular hotel chains there. This will talk about your competitors and the preference of your customers or consumers at a time of choosing a hotel or their preferred hotel. A summary, market research answers to why. Why would you choose this hotel rather than the other? Why would you like to purchase this product even if it's more expensive? It uses observation and surveys to create personas to target your audience, to segment your audience through other techniques like focus groups. You can understand the likelihood of your products or services to succeed. Market research is an instrumental analytical piece because it takes you closer to why your customers behave in a certain way. In the next chapter, Statistics.

# Statistics

Welcome to the statistics chapter. Statistics is probably one of the oldest analytics methodologies. In fact, the history of statistics in a modern way goes back to the 18th century in Germany. Yet statistics are still very much used by businesses. When we talk about statistics, we're basically speaking about math. There are two types of statistics, applied for business.

One of them is descriptive. The other is inferential, descriptive statistics. Helps describe, show or summarize data in a meaningful way. For example, your company can use statistics to determine the average salary across all the employees. There are two types of measures. Again, within statistics there are measures of central tendency. Those describe the central position of a frequency distribution for a group of data. We use metrics like mode, median and mean. The second group are measures of spread. These are ways of summarizing a group of data by describing how spread out the scores are. We use ranges, quartiles, deviations and variances to describe measures of spread. Inferential Statistics are techniques that allow us to use data samples to make generalizations about bigger populations.

For example, government service uses a sample of the population to determine the average salary of the entire nation. They take a group of data that is big enough to extrapolate it to the entire country. Applications of statistics, financial analysis, production, operations. It uses data sets and data warehouses, tools. One very popular, SPSS by IBM. But in recent years, R programming languages, Of course, Excel. And SAS. As usual Best practices are data quality and statistical significance to ensure accuracy of the statistics models.

How can we apply statistics to your hotel chain? Using descriptive statistics, we could determine what are the same patterns during week or weekend. So we can see that during the week, the average stays 2.5 days with a median of two. On weekends, Visitors stay for 0.93 on average. Obviously, since the weekend has only two days. The median will be one and the standard deviation will be only one. Applying inferential statistics. Help us, for example, understand what these patterns are on a bigger level, applied to a bigger group, a bigger population?

Have a look at the chart on the It uses inferential statistics to determine what is the occupancy rate worldwide by region. They have surveyed. They have asked for the data for a group of hotels in each region and they have extrapolated these numbers to the entire population. So you can see the ups and downs of the hotels. And it is very curious to see here in the Asia Pacific. This was the start of the Covid coronavirus spread in Asia and the consequent drop in the occupancy rates. Statistics summarizes data, both descriptive and inferential rely on the same data set. However, descriptive statistics rely solely on these datasets.

Whilst inferential statistics also rely on these data to make generalizations to extrapolate it to a larger population. Statistics help you summarize data and also in fair results to larger populations using sampling like that and linking it back to market research. You can, for example, survey a small portion of your hotel guests and extrapolate the results to your entire customer base in the next chapter, econometrics.

# Econometrics

Congratulations on making it to the last chapter in this chapter, Econometrics. Econometrics, Is the application of mathematical and statistical methods to describe economic systems. It's the use of math and stats to quantify economic phenomena. The applications are calculation of inflation at a macro economic level. Financial strategy or predict, detect or measure changes in economy. Three types of data are mainly used cross-chapteral time series and pooled data. The common use tools are SPSS, R, eViews and STATA.

The best practices and techniques used are regression models, correlations and estimations. So how can we apply econometrics to your hotel? What will be your hotel demand in response to a price change? For example, if we decrease prices, you might increase your revenue by 10 percent. But it may be the case that if you increase prices, demand falls and your revenue will drop by five percent. Looking at the chart on the right, you can see that using the hotel datasets, there is a positive correlation between bookings and average daily rate.

What that means in a nutshell is that if you change prices, it's very likely that your bookings will also change. These two metrics, these two measures are highly correlated. Econometrics is economy applied statistics. It is used to predict inflation or GDP at a macro level. For businesses, it's used to establish correlations between two or more variables like price and demand. In the next chapter, you will start learning about the second big group of data practices, you will sneak peek into the future. with predictive analytics.

# Predictive Models

Welcome back. In the next two chapters, we enter the topic of advanced analytics, which refers to predictive and prescriptive analytics. These two are very trendy and they are usually performed by data scientists. They also present more complexity than descriptive analytics because you need the solid data foundation and advanced skills to achieve meaningful and actionable results. Many companies are investing heavily in advanced analytics with the purpose of making accurate decisions and creating bulletproof strategies.

In this chapter, you will learn about Predictive models. What is a predictive model? Predictive modeling refers to the process of using known results to create, process and validate a model that can be used to forecast future outcomes. It analyzes fixed historical data to increase the probability of forecasting events. Understand customer behavior as well as financial, economic and market risks. Some applications of predictive models are demand forecasting. How's gonna be my demand in the future, workforce planning, how much people do I need in the factory or in the hotel, churn analysis, fleet or equipment maintenance, modeling credit and other financial risks Predictive modeling usually or normally a lot of data, and they rely on the data coming from data warehouse and applying machine learning, algorithms, through tools like Hadoop, R and Python.

Some of the best practices are using regression or applying random forests algorithms. But there are some challenges in predictive modeling. You will need enough data, comprehensive data sets. You need to adapt your models to new problems at the time of building a model. There are factors that you might not be considering because they are not part of the current situation. So the models need to be able to adapt to new situations. I will give you a very simple example. Many companies had to rework all their models based on the Covid to the coronavirus crisis that happened in 2020, because when they build a model that didn't happen and that is a big factor to change behaviors and shopping and what customers are doing around your brands. Data organization and hygiene, summarizes in that data has to have quality and Of course, data privacy and security.

The model's list respects the privacy laws and the security of the data that it's being used. If we look up the lifecycle and simplify it into three steps, a predictive model starts gathering data. The data from the past is collected, prepared, transformed and put it in a manner that can be then applied on top of the algorithm, can be applied on top of the data, in the third step, The model is built, the model produced some results and when possible, embedded into the system to optimize performance. Some of the models that you build might have an ad hoc one off use. Some others will be integrated into systems like, for example, credit scoring algorithms, process data. And whenever you submit an application for a loan or a credit, they process all your data to give back in return.

The result of the predictive algorithm is positive or negative or requires more information. As you have seen, predictive models can forecast what will probably happen in the future, but they present some challenges. Data needs to be available and it has to be accurate. Another important point is privacy concerns.

Concerns like the GDPR, or General Data Protection Regulation in Europe pushes data practices to be respectful and transparent with the data of customers. Let's see, how can predictive modeling be used for the benefit of the business?

Let's look at some example recommendation systems. These recommendation systems are algorithms that use data to suggest additional products or services to consumers based on a variety of reasons and a variety of different variables. If we look at Netflix, one of the most popular broadcasters and On-Demand platforms of video nowadays, the recommendation system works in a way that every time that you start watching something or you spend a certain time watching something on Netflix, this data is collected and informs the algorithm. Then, based on these choices and other factors, like at what time, for example, like what time you watch it or what is your gender They offer you personalized recommendations. Up to 75% of what consumers watch on Netflix comes from the company's recommender system.

And if you look at the right side of this chart, we are going to use a measure that is called Effective Effective catalog size, which talks about the consumption of the catalog of a platform right, for a company. For example, Netflix wants you to watch more than more than one series or one documentary. The more that you watch, the more effective use of the catalog size. What is interesting is that in the cases where the content is personalized and then Netflix is offering you suggestions, the use of the catalogs is four times higher. Then when it's not, that helps Netflix not only optimize revenues, but also produce more series, series and content, knowing that it's going to be used by their consumers. Let's talk about scoring, scoring. It's a model in which there are several variables.

Again, data points are weighted and result in a score. This score is then used to form the basis for a decision. We see this allowed in leads. When companies are working with leads and want to get new business to true leads to potential new customers, they are using predictive analytics to produce a score. DocuSign, the leading company in digital documents and signatures produced the predictive lead scoring to transition from a letter grade ranking system ABC D to a purchasing likelihood percentage of this customer or this lead. Sorry, it's 80 percent likely to purchase Docusign. So what people are doing with the salespeople at Docusign is that they're using these days to focus on these prospects with high probability of becoming customers.

The time is limited. They cannot call 600 people every day. So they get in touch with the customers that are more likely to become customers. That resulted in a 38 percent increase in qualified leads for DocuSign. Churn is defined as when a customer stops using the services of a company, for example, going back to the Netflix that we said before. If I cancel my subscription with Netflix, I churn. So churn analysis in a company has become of key importance. There is a small example here and you can see how drastic the numbers change in terms of number of customers or subscribers for a one percent churn.

Where we are at like 4500 customers here and when we move to 2.5%, there is a dramatic decrease to less than 2,000 consumers. And in the following, starting in the 60 months, that's why companies are like telcos, investing a lot in churn models to use to build these models. They use information like customers, what's the zip code? Where do they exactly live? What is their gender? What do they do? The occupation? What type of products are they buying? Did they purchase through a coupon? Did they purchase frequently? What was the last time they renewed the subscription or purchased a new product? And consumer's interactions like a complaint, complaint is usually a key driver for customers to churn.

If someone called repeatedly to the telecommunications company complaining about their his/her bills. It's likely that at some point they will stop/cease their relationship with this company. A Churn success story. A leading equity broker had a problem because 35 percent of their consumers were churning/stopped trading after generating some losses. So they created an analytical model that predicted the price range at which investors are likely to sell stocks based on the trading patterns. So with all this information, they managed to achieve a seven percent account reactivation. So users that had churned came back to the platform to continue trading. Risk management is used by banks and other financial entities to evaluate the risk of approving a loan, a mortgage or similar. Other companies use it to forecast and avoid unpaid bills and overdue bills as well.

In this example, do the second largest telecom provider of the United Arab Emirates was in the need of retaining good customers and most importantly, reduce the rollovers of customers into collection They created the model for onboarding and customer management that also resulted in policy strategies for credit limit management and early stage collection to increase their own time payments by 30 percent using this model and reduce their past few accounts by 22 percent. In maintenance, The use of predictive maintenance determines the condition of in-service equipment in order to estimate when the maintenance should be performed, as opposed to the traditional methods that are time based or routine based.

The leading company, the National Finnish railway operator. VR group successfully solved the problem of maintenance in two phases. Firstly, deploying in their trains, sensors that collect data and report back on the condition of the parts. And secondly, building a mathematical model that predicts which parts are likely to fail so they can be replaced before the cost of unplanned downtime. Think about a train that is broken because one of the wheels is broken. But the train would have been repaired yesterday. This train will continue moving and will keep servicing passengers. All this resulted in a 33 percent reduction in maintenance work for VR. Applied to your hotels.

Let's go back to your hotel. So predicting booking cancellations. We saw previously that we can estimate the number of booking cancellations based on history. But if we add more variables, we will be able to more accurately understand which kind of bookings are likely to be canceled right when they are made. You have a column, a chart here with four hotels at the bottom, H1, H2, H3 and H4, and the variables that have been used to build this model. And in the darker colors, you'll appreciate it. What are these data points? These variables have a big impact in cancellations of reservations. You can see in that country for Hotel one, not so much for hotel two the required parking spaces for again, hotel one and some others like data room type in Hotel four, are critical for customers, for guests to cancel their booking right away.

Putting these together and with a robust model for your hotel, can now integrate these to avoid cancellations with complementary offers. If you know that the booking is likely to be canceled, you can take actions to avoid this cancellation beforehand. You can book the same room more than once, overbooking, or you can improve your cancellation policies. You can see on the right that some of these algorithms can achieve a very high accuracy rate, like this one is close to one percent in H1 and H2. Very, very close to one percent. So this is a reliable metric measure to tell you if a booking. It's likely to be canceled. Predictive models predict how likely things are to happen in the future. They use as many variables as possible to be effective.

The more data points that compute, the more likely that they will be accurate. They are adopted by many industries and fields to predict energy saving, risk, failures, Quality of leads or churn. Predictive models are really powerful tool. and Their applications are infinite. You can predict when your hotel is going to be full or when the washing machines will break. This is why so many companies are investing a lot in hiring data scientists and building models. But at the same time, it poses some challenges.

Many times it roadblocks like lack of quality or data privacy issues, predictive analytics becomes almost a mission impossible. If there is no solid data foundation. Another important task is to create clear goals, milestones for your predictive models using questions like what are we willing to do to change the Book of action? Or how will we shape our strategy based on what's likely to happen in the future. In the next chapter, you will learn about Data Mining

# Data Mining

In this chapter, you will learn about data mining. As the term suggests, this approach looks at finding meaningful patterns across large and complex datasets. Data mining is the process of finding anomalies, patterns and correlations within large datasets to predict outcomes. Data mining. Automates the extraction of meaningful data from large and complex data sets. Using one or more softwares. Data mining is applied in health care, educational CRM, fraud detection, research and in general in any field that produces large amounts of data. The data is commonly stored in data warehouses and again applies Machine learning algorithms, Rapid Miner, R and Python are used and there are some best practices that apply to data mining that the data must be maintained at the more granular level.

The data must not be archived or deleted. Data must be timestamped. Semantics of the data must be consistent and the data must not be overwritten. Let's look at some data mining techniques, tracking patterns. In our hotel dataset, for example. Breakfast appears frequently. 77% of the occurrences linked to a reservation. A subsequence Could be those that book breakfast, also book parking. So there is a clear pattern between bookings and breakfast. Classification, It collects various attributes together into categories which you can use then to draw further. The conclusion is some sort of labeling, classifying.

For example, you've seen the predictive model that we build for cancellations. In the previous chapter, we can classify our bookings into high, medium or low risk of cancellation

Association. It's when you look for specific events or attributes that are highly correlated with another event or attribute. You might find, for example, in your hotel that customers that book a weekend also book half board. This is also what normally powers that people also bought in chapters of the online stores, items that they frequently bought together. Outlier Detection in many cases, You also need to be able to identify anomalies or outliers in your data.

Looking at the picture on the right side and getting it from our reservation data from your hotel, there is a date where the cancellations spiked up, spiking up to almost 1,500. You probably want to investigate what drove it. So this is a good example of detection of an outlier. Clustering is very similar to classification, but involves grouping different chunks of data together based on their similarities. For example, you might want to cluster different demographics of your guests into different buckets like adults and children or market segment. These different market segments have been clustered to show the percentage of reservations that they produce. And here you can see the adults versus children.

In summary, data mining tries to find patterns in large or complex data sets that helps focus on meaningful parts of the data. It is very helpful for companies that collect large data sets and attributes like telecommunications, banks, insurance, hotels or airlines. Now, you know why Data Mining received its name, it is literally like trying to find gold. When you have one or multiple large data sets in front of you. Data mining will help you find the important parts And so get rid of the noise around. Through techniques like clustering or association. We can easily group large chunks of data and pay attention to important events. In the next chapter, Text Analytics.

# Text Analytics

Text Analytics has become trendy in the last five to 10 years with the explosion of data originated by platforms like Facebook or Reddit. And usually in the form of comments, forums or reviews, companies are in the need to understand what users are saying about them, analyzing and understanding a larger amount of text started to be a burden for companies as they had to use a lot of resources to read. In many cases, one by one, all the comments or reviews that their customers had left on the Internet. Was then that the science of data came to the rescue with algorithms that can read Classify And understand millions of comments in multiple languages.

Text Analytics. It's the automated process of translating large volumes of unstructured text into quantitative data to uncover insights, trends and patterns. Text analytics is also known as text mining or text analysis. Most data mining techniques apply as well as date for text analytics. Text analytics is using sentiment analysis. Voice of consumer, feedback. Also heavy use in the spam filters and things like national security. Governments listen to a lot of information to know If you are trying to do things that are not legal. It received data from data warehouses, but also API's machine learning and uses NLP tools like IBM Watson, Discovery Text, Google Cloud NLP, Amazon, Comprehend and Python. And the best practices are semantic based engines.

A native translations and annotations. But how can text analytics help companies? Only in 2019, Internet users posted half a million new tweets. Half a million new comments on Facebook and send 188 millions emails every minute. Managing and analyzing all this information becomes a challenge. But thanks to text analytics, businesses are able to automatically extract meaning from all sorts of text data. Social media posts, emails, live chats and service and turn it into insights. Some text analytics techniques are sentiment analysis. It's the interpretation of classifications, of emotions usually translated into positive, negative and neutral. How do customers feel about your hotel?

You can see some reviews in the form of text and the algorithm that returns the analysis to sentiment analysis. Amazing location is positive. The air condition makes so much noise negative and neutral. An example could be the outside of the hotel is under construction. It will look beautiful when it's done. It's not positive nor negative. It's just a statement. Term frequency defines how frequently a word appears in a text and its importance relative to the whole set of the text. For example, if you take your customer calls from the calls that they make to your hotel and you transcribe them. You can group common words in calls related to their hotel like location, room types or breakfast. This is usually what produced the so-called word of clouds. What are the words?

The frequency that my customers I mention in when they call the call center. Topic modeling. It's a form of classification that helps groups in two different categories. The type of text that we are analyzing If you look at the right hand side, I would like to change my booking. This probably belongs to reservations. Could you send me an invoice? Payments. Do you serve vegetarian food? This is a food and beverage query. Can I pay by credit card? This is payments again. Could you install a cot for a baby in the room? Special request. And how much is the breakfast per person? Food and Beverage. Grouping All these emails, calls into these topics. Help us build things like FAQs or create a knowledge base for your customer care agents and provide the right answers in less time to their customers that call. Named Entity Recognition. It's a technique that looks like a recognizing noun and could be used to extract persons, organizations, geographic locations, dates, monetary amounts, etc..

I wrote the text and I use an NER engine and this is under explosion.ai And if you see I wrote here a brief text and automatically the algorithm recognizes that this is a person and I am from Spain and I'm talking about a percentage and that I would like to make an appointment with you. This is a date and ordinal and again a date. This is also a kind of algorithm that is heavily used for web scraping. This is how machines identify your name and your email and fetch it from a comment or a post that you did somewhere.

A summary is that text analytics algorithms can process vast amounts of text and classify it, analyze the sentiment and even recognize the cardinality of specific words, like we just saw. It's very used for social media, web scraping and voice of consumer reviews, customer care calls or emails. Text Analytics is an impressive technique that will help you analyze millions of words with a few clicks. You can understand what the text talks about, if there are consistently repeated words or if the person who wrote it has a positive or negative feeling.

Today, machine learning algorithms are constantly learning new languages and expressions with the aim of better understanding the human language. You're Google Home or Alexa, learning every time you talk to them to offer you the best experience Natural Language Processing. It's the engine that processes all that information. Also, text analytics is a great input for other data and analytics disciplines like predictive modeling. I hope that you have enjoyed this chapter of the Book. In the next one, you will discover some of the latest trends in the use of data with Prescriptive Analytics

# Computer Vision

Welcome to the chapter, prescriptive analytics, prescriptive analytics is the area of data analytics that focuses on finding the best Book of action in a scenario using available data. Prescriptive analytics is the natural progression from descriptive and predictive analytics procedures. It goes a step further to answer the question of what I should do. In this chapter, You will learn about the most advanced analytics techniques. You will see how artificial intelligence is applied to business and in your daily life. We will start with computer vision.

Computer Vision is a field of study that seeks to develop techniques to help computers see. And also understand the content of digital images like videos and photographs. It could be broadly called a subfield of artificial intelligence and machine learning. And then make use of general learning algorithms. It is using virtual reality, predictive maintenance, health care and more and more in the automotive industry. It's basically sources, images and videos used as tools like OpenCV and Matlab. And some of the best practices are Image resizing. Object detection and identification and Landmark detection. Now we will see a few techniques within the field of computer vision. Object classification, what category of object is in this photograph? Animals. Object identification.

Which type of object is in this photograph? Giving a category to animals? These are cats. Object verification is the object in the photograph. Is the cat in the photograph? This is what powers the famous capture and recapture images that sometimes you need to accept to continue and visit or register in a Web site. Object detection. What are the objects in the photograph? This practice, this approach is fundamental for the automotive industry and driverless cars. Object landmine detection. What are the key points and where are they in the photograph?

As you might have guessed, this is the technology used to provide weather effects in the video calls and chats and Instagram and Snapchat and all these social media applications, object segmentation. What pixels belong to the object in image? It's tracing the silhouette and defining what is the surface they did in the area that is covering each one of the objects in the image object recognition. What exact objects are in this photograph and what are they? What kind of code do we have in the center? What kind of coke is on the left? Computer vision for business. Tesla, the popular car manufacturer, uses computer vision heavily in their cars. They rely heavily on deep learning and computer vision algorithms.

You can see here on the right hand side what a Tesla car, the computer the machine sees when someone is driving. They are not getting the full point of replacing human drivers, but they are very close to it. In fact, in the chapter, you can see that the person that is on the steering wheel is doing absolutely nothing. His dad is just there for legal reasons because as of today, cars are not allowed to drive autonomously without a driver. In health care, computer vision technology can detect abnormalities in imagery derived from MRI and C.A.T. scans with a higher degree of accuracy than medical professionals. This is not to diminish the experience and good cause of the medical doctors, but it seems that good items and computer vision can help detect to a much higher grade of accuracy something that is in an MRI. There is no wonder that radiologists, cardiologists, and oncologists have embraced computer vision as a companion in their day to day work in industry.

More and more foreign manufacturers are adding cameras, as you can see in the picture, to their production line. They identify defective products on the production line, inspect equipment to do predictive maintenance. Not only that defective products, but it also enhances the coupé. I wanted to have a look at all these bottles. Look at the level of liquid in all of them. And then look at this one. This will be picked by the camera and through the algorithm, an anomaly will be reported. Then the machine can be adjusted to put the right amount of liquid in each bottle. Retailer Amazon go. I'm gonna leave you with a chapter.

Four years ago, we started to wonder. What would shopping look like if you could walk into a store, grab what you want and just go? What if we could weave the most advanced machine learning computer vision and A.I. into the very fabric of a store? So you never have to wait in line. No lines, no checkouts, no registers. Welcome to Amazon. Go use Amazon. Go back to enter. Then put away your phone and start shopping. It's really that simple. Take whatever you like. Anything you pick up is automatically added to your virtual car. If you change your mind about that cupcake, just put it back. Our technology will update your virtual card automatically. So how does it work? We used computer vision, deep learning algorithms and sensor fusion, much like you'd find in self-driving cars.

We call it just walk out technology. Once you've got everything you want, you can just go when you leave, ah, just walk out. Technology adds up your virtual card and charges your Amazon account. Your receipt is sent straight to the app and you can keep going. No lines, no Check-Out. No, seriously. Amazon used several technologies related to computer vision and machine learning in the Amazon go shops to start. They use special detection. Remember the detection? They identify that you're a human. Your shape, where you are and where each person is in the store. They do this to a network of cameras. Then they recognize the different items that are sold.

This is what lets you lift the shop without going through a cashier. They both estimate where the person is near a shelf. And what are they doing with their arms? And then finally, the activity analysis determines whether you picked something or you returned it with all this together. The algorithm can predict very, very accurately the items that you have in your bag. And then when you leave the shop that you have left and charge in your credit card the amount of your grocery. In summary, computerization helps computers see and understand images and videos.

The information is then processed to detect, recognize and classify images and videos. It is supplied in virtual reality for anomaly detection in health care and power. Driverless cars. Impressive. What technology can do, what is powered by data? I hope that you understand the essence of computer vision for us humans. It's very easy to possess images all the time before computers even deputize. That's a scary thing. That's a good sign. It has to be beneficial. I think aims at detecting tumors are the features in his car accidents and that this cost in the next chapter of operations research.

# Operations Research

Historically, the term operations research originated during the Second World War, when the U.S. and Great Britain armed forces sought the assistance of scientists to solve complex and very difficult strategic and tactical problems of warfare operations research. It's a discipline that uses mathematical, statistical and algorithms to model and solve complex problems. Data mining, the optimal solution and improving decision making. This matter is also called operational research decision science or management science.

The applications of operational research are supply chain enterprise resource planning, inventory management. They pull data from data, our houses, data sets, Internet of Things devices or API as tools like g. B. K. R or Rapid Minor are frequently used and among the best practices we find meaning or problem in Q A.S. sequined see problems and network analysis. What is the process of operations research identifying a problem that needs to be solved. This is usually recurrent problems that many businesses and companies face and that they try to solve. Then a model is constructed around the problem and the mother resembles the real world and puts and puts impossible variables.

The model is then used to derive solutions to the problem. So a few solutions are identified right after their solutions are tested and techniques like a B testing or multivariate testing to test each one of the solutions or piloting. And finally, the solution is to implement and hopefully if the testing is successful. The problem is fixed. So we go from identifying a problem to a data model. We use the model to create. So find solutions. Solutions are tested and solutions are deployed. They are put in place. So how can operations research how businesses linear programming? It's a very frequent technique used for deliveries and for companies that do services with routing.

If you look at the chart on the right and considering that this is your warehouse and you need to deliver five packages to each one of these houses, considering the time between them and that you obviously want to save fuel and time taking the shortest route groats linear programming, help you calculate the different routes and choose the shortest route to serve all the packages. They do all the old all your deliveries. This process is again called linear programming. But this is not necessarily the shirtdress. It's not necessarily the best of the roads because there may be other variables that will impact your deliveries. There may be a certain time where you can not deliver house number five because they want delivery in the afternoon and you are out in the morning or something like that.

Anything can happen. More variables should be inputted. But so is the process of choosing the best, the best Grote. In general, it's called the operations research. So we make the decision here between linear programming, the shortest route and the best route operations, research, queuing in retail, for example. Let's say that your retail location has increasing traffic. And in the late afternoon and you see that you are getting cues and some of the cues are forcing customers to wait up to 10 minutes. You need to come up with a solution and a potential solution will bring or we'd put one more capturing in the line. But that has a cost as well. And you might need to find a balance between the day, the day, the time that the users wait in the queue and the amount of money that you're spending and you cash in in your head count. This is where models are applied for operational research to estimate the right balance between, for example, employees and the waiting time.

You might reach a solution that has an average of five minutes. Wait for everyone, but it's not CEDO time. See waiting time, because that would be very. For you, putting in a lot of cash, yes. Inventory management. Another frequent problem that a company faces, how much inventory should I order on my way into much? Some parts of the inventory are selling quickly. How much stock I'm carrying, which inventory is increasing my holding costs, or how can I make sure that I have what I need at any time? Because you want to have products when you need them, but you don't want to overstock, you don't want to hoard products because that elevates your costs. Replacement is another topic where operational research is very active. Things that deteriorate with time like machines, vehicles, or it could be in buildings. You also have items that become out of date because there are new technologies.

For example, you need to replace your computers or cameras with new cameras that bring new functionalities. There are other sets of items that do not deteriorate, but they fade completely after a certain amount of use. See the example on the right of a bulb. A bulb. Stop working and then it's done. And also the existing working stuff and enabling organization staff at some point to start retiring or having low performance and they churn or other things can happen. So a replacement is another area where operations research can help. Now, let's have a look at your hotels and then a specific business and operations research. How can we apply linear programming, remember?

What's the best road in housekeeping, for example? This is a question that many hotels and believe me, I have worked in the hotel industry are wondering everyday and employees. Which room do we clean first so that we make sure that the employee or the valet has time to clean all the rooms. There is no time wasted, but there is also no stress in our overtime because you are late to clean some room. So one of the questions could be, should I start with rooms that are vacant today or those at our exits? When we look at queuing, there is a very clear example. It is very similar to what we saw before the reception. We all have seen our hotel that after a flight or a bus came in, has a very long queue of people waiting in the reception.

Now, you cannot have infinite reception waiting for a peak of 10 minutes. So how much are you willing your customers to wake versus how much stuff do you want to hire for that specific peak time in terms of you mentally? Another case that happens frequently in hotels. It's an amenity. If you buy in bulk, you will have better prices. If you buy all the shampoo and the towels and everything bad, you can pile up in stock, stock price and stocking and also some of your products and especially in the and be food and beverage part can expire replacement.

Super important things for hotels. When is the right time to refurbish your hotel or the rooms or the lobby or redo the reception. These kinds of things, these refineries and reconstruction supporters are very expensive. So you might want to make sure that you do it at the right time. The value of your hotel decreases and it gets older. That's a fact. And you want to know when the value has decreased enough for you to close some parts of the hotel or some areas of their areas of the hotel and start reconstructing it to gain again this value of a new hotel or a new refurbished hotel.

Let's see a summary of this chapter, operations research is about recommending the best action to optimize business performance. It has important uses for cue and inventory management, sequential tasks, efficiency and replacements are also used by many listeners. Operational research has some similarities with the victims' mothers. In fact, there is some overlap between them. We can summarize specific and recurring business questions that many organizations face by inventory.

# Signal Processing

DSP, or digital signal processing is a range between analog and digital worlds. And today we're learning how you're using it often in your daily life. ASPEY or digital signal processing is the process of analyzing and modifying a signal to optimize or improve its efficiency. It involves applying mathematical and computational algorithms to analog and also digital signals to produce a signal that is of higher quality. How is DSP used?

The USPS is heavily used in the hearing industry. Right, as well as the music industry. So the noise canceling headphones, for example, and hearing devices that people with hearing problems use are powered by the speed. The way it works is that the analog sound, it's inputted into the device. Then the process, this digital process, digital signals process and a safety in a memory to end up producing a digital sound of higher quality. This is how your noise canceling headphones reduce the noise they get to initially sound from whatever device that you are connected to. They clean up, they apply the algorithm, the signal processing on top to deliver.

And the output is a sound that doesn't have noise around. It is also used in a speech recognition system like Google Home or Alexa uses your voice and in increasing the quality of your voice and preparing your voice to enable what we will see later. And it would be natural language processing as well as in translation and dictation. Hi. This is an example of the S.P. in practice. I am talking to my computer and the text is reaching the screen.

Digital signal processing is about acquiring and enhancing mostly analog inputs.

It is used for audio compression, image and video compression, speech recognition, seismology sonar or radar technology. DSD has many applications for data analytics, recommending we improve the quality of image or stock in things like detecting earthquakes, goalie or love, nice company. And then the next chapter image process.

# Image Processing

Digital age processing is a subset of digital single processing that we saw in the last chapter, however, and due to its importance, there is a chapter dedicated exclusively to the processing and enhancements of HS. Image processing consists of the manipulation of images using computers. Computer algorithms get an image enhanced and extract useful information from them. Some of the applications are image compression. Computer vision. Microscopic image in an image restoration. It obviously uses images of every kind. There are tools, some of them very famous, like Photoshop or any other image editing software. But others are more advanced and sophisticated like Matlab and Python.

Some of the best practices enhancement, color processing, compression, segmentation and a technique called wavelets applied in real life image restoration is one of the most obvious and clear aspects are our uses of image processing. How does this happen? Similarly to the digital signal processing an image, its input into a computer. Then the algorithms calculate all the points and vectors of the image so they can recalculate them afterwards and enhance or modify the image. These enhancements or modifications are starting a memory and the result is an enhanced image.

This is what is used in things like image filtering where you have an Instagram or any other social media application that allows you to edit images on the fly. Basically they're computing using an algorithm, your image, your original source image, or, for example, the unlocking features that many phones have nowadays. They will recognize the image, recognize that it is you, and then unlock your device. A quick summary data.

The digital image processing is a widely used data analytics technique, cameras editing southwards and social media used to modify and improve the quality of. Image processing is embedded in our lives. Photo Energis, Instagram. The iPhone. All of them are used in each state in the process here.

# Natural Language Processing

You saw me go and I'll be in the ladies password selector at the beginning of the Book, natural language processing is the size that makes computers understand the human language. Natural language processing, usually shortened as entropy, is a branch of artificial intelligence that deals with the interaction between computers and humans using their natural language. The objective of entropy is to rate, decipher, understand and make sense of the human languages in a manner that is valuable and will be applied heavily in language, translation, word processors, interactive voice response IVR and personal assistant personal assistant applications. They use text and Bow Street voice recordings and anything derived from text or human language. Python.

It's very much used in an LP, but also there are other tools like Gore LP or text. Some of the best practice syntax, the semantics and tokenization I was to apply to your daily life. We said at the beginning and the digital signal processing that this DSP improves the quality of your voice to produce a higher quality signal that is an input to your personal assistant. But is energy the natural language processing the one that understands? And send your comments to the assistant. Word processors use NLB to correct, suggest or improve your writing. They apply semantic rules and deep learning to understand the meaning. Tone and Atrous in your text on the right hand side are quite popular.

The text editor and Deuce's enter Peko Gramley. That is really good at understanding what you're writing and suggesting the best way of writing it. How can we apply entropy to your hotels? Translation translation devices are becoming common in hotel reception. Maybe you have come across some of these. I've seen hotels using Google home to translate what customers are saying in real time. Imagine that now you can receive and accommodate requests from guests all over the world and not only the languages that your staff might speak, I.B. hours or interactive voice responses. These are their famous robots that talk to you when you call a call center or you want to complain or to request or to buy something through the telephone for good. They are now the first call off response when you call a hotel. And thanks to NLB, your customers no longer need to type on the phone by describing the requests and the machine can best serve it.

Let's see an example where Someone is calling to ask something, And the first question that the IBRD machine asks is if they have a reservation or not. If there is any, decide to do some modifications to the reservation. And after describing the request and understanding what the customer wants, they will be transferred to the front desk that can help them with their request or help him or her with the request of getting an extra bed for their room. It's also for companies. It's a way to save time and money on a lot of front desk stuff.

And a piece about analyzing and understanding human language is the algorithms to compute and learn from human voice or text to provide answers, personal assistance, translation or interactive voice responses. Some of the use of some of these. An MP has been gone for the last two years. The possibility of making computers understand, as we say, is more important. But let's take action. I hope in an infinite world of possibilities, it also opens in practice submissions, listening and learning from everything that makes mistakes. And in the next chapter, there are mistakes.

# Metaheuristics

Welcome back. In this short chapter, we will have a look at Marius's before we start talking about Mata Hari Stix. We will see what the meaning of heuristics is. Heuristics are methods for solving problems in a quick way that delivers a result that is sufficient enough to be useful given the time constraints. But here is this can lead to poor decision making based on a limited data set. But the speed of decisions can sometimes make up for this habit. Just this is a clear example where you don't have all the data that you need to make an 100 percent informed decision or to have a 100 percent accurate model. But he still wants to use this data to make a decision that is approximate to something that could happen in reality. It's an approximation.

If someone will dress this in their office, you probably quickly think that this is weird, but maybe you don't know what is the background? What is she dressing like these or what is behind her behavior or what is the dressing? This is what we call a risk taker. You take a quick conclusion based on a fact, but do you not necessarily have all the evidence is with you? What is made of ray sticks is a high level problem, independent algorithm framework that provides for the strategies to develop heuristic optimization. I got Adam's. So what is the difference here, ethics are problem dependent. You define a heretic for a given problem. What does matter? Heuristics are a problem.

Independent techniques that can be applied to a broad range of problems is a framework to take holistic based decisions. He made a few mistakes. Are using genetes, particle swarm optimization, resource planning and deliberate routing to their source data from the usual suspects that are houses, data sets, Internet of Things API is. Python is quite used here. For some matahari sticks and some best practices are a single solution versus population based hybridization and mimetic algorithms. One example of Mayta here, mystic's or holistic is a traveling salesman problem which asks the following.

Giving a list of cities and the distances between each pair of cities. What is the shortest possible road that visits each city and returns to the Origin City? Now the problem here is that the search space at the candidate, the solutions as he moves, grows faster than exponentially as the size of the problem increases. What we're trying to say is that the more solutions that we find, the more than you expand. The data said your problem is bigger and bigger. We've mentioned DNA before in age and in genetics because it's also a problem with the genetic code being so large that finding a close solution, an exact solution, it's literally impossible or impossible, as we said here.

In summary, Matahari sticks are frameworks to try to approximate solutions to huge, big problems that are complex. We have now reached the end of a chapter with the State Department ethics. I hope you find it useful. Corporate takeovers, many of the techniques and approaches in this chapter complement. And in some cases overlap with others. Think in cases using computer vision, not for a lack of trust in this process to keep machines the ability to see this and talk and execute in the next model. We will look at a few key aspects of data based on data.

# Data Architecture

Why go to the model data management in the following four chapters? You will learn about some aspects that are fundamental for data analytics, architecture, quality master data and data privacy. Without that, neither descriptive, predictive or prescriptive analytic would be possible. Let's see what data architecture is. It's a set of rules, policies, standards and models that govern and define the type of data collected and how it is used.

Start managed and integrated within an organization and its database systems. Some components of data architecture are data processing, cloud storage applications, encryption and network. We will see a few, a few of them in detail in a second. The infrastructure that architects usually design and consider our data warehouses API is F.T. piece. And so I like it. Some famous tools are popular, there are many data architecture tools. But Oracle powered design and an artist studio are often Lee mentioned by architects and best practices, scalability, business alignment and data governance. So what are some of the tasks that the data architectures take on? Access, access and management with this.

Architects are able to identify and authenticate users. Access to data is restricted in organizations. As you know. And are the architects in charge to design the security around all this data cloud storage? Cloud storage is a mother of computer data storage in which digital data is a start. A logical pause. These boards are usually servers as well, located in multiple locations.

And the physical environment, the place where the actual servers leave residue, is hosted, managed by a hosted company. Data Processing Architects take care of the collection and manipulation of items to data to produce meaningful information. There are a few faces in data processing that are in this case, we're going to mention for data collection, data input, data processing and data output.

This entire process is managed by architects' data centers. In this case are data engineers who are involved in the data selection design and the facilities and systems that are part of a data center. Data center is what we said a couple of chapters ago is the physical location of the service that holds the data. It's a place where you have a lot of computers with a lot of harvest's or data systems. They must also know how to operate and maintain electrical cooling and I.T. equipment networks, data architects designed and managed electronic databases to start and organize data. They investigate companies' current data and develop a plan to integrate current systems.

With that, decide features takes how the systems talk to each other, how data is collected from API and dumped into this data warehouses or physical server locations where we store the data of the company, transfer data transfer respect to the collection, replication and transmission of large datasets from one organization to business unit to another. In some cases, architects are in charge of transferring data from one server to another, from one application to the other, replicating data or similar. And encryption encryption is encoding information so that can only be accessed by the users with the correct encryption key. So there is a difference between user access and encryption.

Encryption is how the database is encoded and the user access given to the end user. Eventually the key that can decrypt this data. This is a basic building block of data security and it's a very important step to ensure that all computer assisted information that is in our computers and in servers is protected or from someone that can want to steal it or leaks or this kind of data issues. Last but not least, architects. Also, the sign ups, data visualization apps, visual gauges, gadgets or EDL monitoring tools are some of the examples of applications developed by data architects. Well, you have seen that the architects are taking care of a lot of things. And as you might have imagined, there are different roles within data architecture and engineering.

Architects do not always perform all these tasks or they are different kinds of architects and engineers doing them. Let's have a look at the different roles. So the data architect conceptualizes and visualizes data frameworks. They are in charge of putting order on the data chaos. Remember, we spoke at large organizations might have hundreds and in some cases a few hundred systems generating data at the same time. So how this data is interconnected and talk to each other. This blueprint is designed by the architects that put together the example on the right, the basement and the proper blocks so that data flows in the organization as it should do. Data engineers build and maintain those frameworks that are created by the architects. They also assist architects in building the mentioned frameworks.

Data engineers, as opposed to architects, have deep knowledge in software engineering because they need to actually execute all the blueprints that the architects have done. And for that they need coding and software engineering expertise. DBAs or database administrators include the Planning Installation Configuration, D.S. Migration's performance monitoring, security, troubleshooting and backup and data recovery of databases. DBAs are taking care of the databases. They are making sure that the databases are up, that there is no downtime, that if a user needs access to a particular database, they will give this access. If data needs to be migrated, they make sure that their data is backed up and can be transferred to another database. They are the database watchdogs. Then we have the figure of the data modeler.

Data modelers work with architects to these same databases that meet the organizational needs. So architects. The entire design, the entire blueprint, the entire architecture of a company's data. But the data modelers are in charge of optimizing the databases. So as you can see here on the right hand side, all the relationships are made. They don't. There is no redundancy. So you don't have a few instances of tabletop made of ISIS with the same data here and there and also performance at that time that you need to access the data. The database, it's so modeled in a way that it's fast to access. And as well, the database is how reliable a summary of this chapter is. Data architecture is a vast domain that includes tasks like infrastructure, governance and security.

The data architecture of a company should be aligned and may make the business calls. This is of key importance. I've seen this happening in many companies. The goals of a company are not necessarily always aligned with the data that you are collecting. And what happened after this? Of course, you cannot answer the business questions because the data that you have gathered is not the data that you need. That is not aligned with your business. Go to super important data. Architecture should mimic business goals.

Data architects and engineers are fundamental to the data health of any station man in charge of the important tasks line, and the business goes with the data strategy. Make sure that all the scientific connections and that the data is stored and accessible for the rest of the users, they are responsible for the Florida update in the next episode. You will get the data anyway.

# Data Quality

If I can help to name one element that is indispensable in data analytics. Apart from the data itself, it will be data, David, why? It's important because we know high quality data. All your analytics efforts can be in vain. Imagine a sales report that shows no numbers on a predictive model with very low accuracy because the data is not complete. For example, any decisions taken are not accurate. Insights can be catastrophic. That is why Congress put so much effort in obtaining high quality data quality. It's planning, implementing and controlling the activities like quality management techniques to data in order to assure it is fit for consumption and meet the needs of data consumers.

Components of data quality are basically anything that is related to reporting analytics, descriptive, predictive and prescriptive analytics data. Prediction has a huge impact in any analytical activity. The infrastructure, it's as useful to all the data that we can collect in the form of coming from data warehouses, API data sets and any other kind of data tools that they get of data quality talent, Informatica data, quality IBM, Foth Infosphere or SCDP Data Services, best practices and data quality data governance data auditing processes and data stigwood in providing with a single source of truth.

Let's have a look at the different dimensions of data quality, how data quality is measured and when do we say that data is of quality? The six hour accuracy, completeness, consistency, integrity, timeliness and uniqueness. Let's have a look at each one of them. Accuracy refers to when the data values that you have in an object or in a data set are correct or not. The values must be the right volume and must be represented in a consistent and unambiguous, not ambiguous form. If you look on the right, Mary seems to have been born two times in a month. It doesn't exist, right? This data is not accurate. Moving on into completeness, I think it's pretty self-explanatory. But we expect comprehensiveness of the data, Data can be complete even if optional data is missing.

As long as the data meet the expectations, then it's considered complete. If we look at the Right-Hand side and in the table, you are expecting to have a price for each one of the home types in your hotel. We are missing a price that should be here. Hence, we can say that this data is not complete. Consistency, consistency means that data across all systems reflect the same information and add in sync with each other. For example, the money in the books should match the money in the bank. All So we have on the right hand side, again, the sales in both hotels in a given month, May of twenty twenty. But the transaction in our ERP or the bank says that we have hundred twenty three thousand. There is a mismatch between data. This data is not consistent across systems. There is data, inconsistency, integrity, data.

Integrity is the overall accuracy, completeness and consistency of data. Data integrity refers to the trustworthiness of data. A balance between the ones that we saw before. But we have an example here of data integrity. We have two different data sets. One of them is the bookings here on top and the other one is the customer names. The reference table, we have a number of booking bookings, I.D., booking reference numbers, and we see that in the third row. We have Peter with the booking number.

Hundred and twenty five in the customer I.D.. Thousand and three. However, in the customer data, said the customer, one hundred and one thousand and three. The reference is not called Peter, but is called Frank. That is contradicting information in this due to databases. So they assume there are integrity issues in this data set. Your data might have integrity issues together with not complete or not accurate.

Another dimension of data quality is timeliness. It refers to the availability and accessibility of data. In making business decisions, how long is the time difference between the data capture and the real world event being captured, for example? Again, looking at the right hand side. If we take today as the 8th of May of 2020 and we look at the data, the last booking number was created in 2019. That is one year lag between data. And today they seem to be a timeliness issue here. This is always the time when the issue is defined by the company policies and the company data architecture. There are companies that expect to have real time data. There are other companies that work with a one day lag data or one month. But in any case, it needs to adhere and adjust to what the company's data architecture and rules are unique.

I think it's pretty clear data should be unique and not duplicated. Data duplication usually brings a lot of problems misreporting Confucians, but aggregations, etc.. I said we have an example on the right where we seem to have two bookings of your hotel that are identical. This data is not unique. What is the cost of data quality board data? Quality is costly. It is, according to Gartner. The average financial impact of that air quality on organizations is nine point seven million dollars per year. IBM also recently discovered that only in the US business is lost three point one trillion annually due to poor data quality.

Let's look at some success stories and how data quality has a real impact on the bottom line of companies. Toby Specking is the UK largest builder, builder, merchant. They have a, quote, data quality firewall that checks for duplicates, confirms that check digits are valid for barcodes, standardize data and produce and product descriptions. So far, they have checked more than half a million products for data quality, and they saw a 30 percent boost in Web site conversion due to, in part, having consistent and accurate printed product description.

You can see on the right hand side how robust and well described their products are. So that bias can have details of what they are purchasing. Customer database quality. This has become the bread and butter of many organizations in terms of data. In this example, Save the Children is reducing duplicates and improving data quality. The charity wants to ensure that the information that it has on individuals is as accurate as possible. For example, if the charity has three records for J. Smith, John Smith and John Smith with Y. It's very likely that this person will receive an email three times. It means that the company will pay three times for email. But even further, the customer can see Camfield himself annoyed for receiving three times the same, the same communication and might want to opt out for helping Save the Children.

A summary of data quality. It's a cornerstone for organizations data analytics, a strategy on data quality for data analytics. Without it, it's very difficult, if not impossible, to do. Descriptive or advanced analytics to data can lead to wrong decisions. You have seen how essential good quality data is for an organization. So I said that more data is worse than no data, but they again tend to run decisions based on value added to my career. I've seen entire data strategies fail and raw data quality. That is why he's stopped. Extreme importance has it under control in the next session. Given that this is massive data.

# Master Data

Suppliers, contracts, products. Measures. Countries. These are businesses of this type of thing. The most valuable agreed upon information is shared across our organization. There remain tables and sometimes static. They were left with masterbate mustered data. It's your business critical data that is stored in systems across your enterprise. Master data is usually non transactional in nature. Some of the applications of master data are Web sites, product catalogs, financial systems, and any system or app that needs to use or reuse gotten constant data sets that are seen frequently in an organization.

The data is used to resource in data warehouses, API data sets or MDA. Ms. Manager must have data management systems. There are tools like Talent, Prophecy, SJP, Ditko or Informatica that are provided with good solutions for data management. And some of the best practices are harmonization, consolidation and applying in business context. Let's see the difference between master data and reference data. We said that master data. It's that piece of data that has common definitions across an organization, a customer.

What is a customer who is a customer? Employees, vendors, suppliers, parts product locations, contact mechanism profiles, accounting items, contracts or policies are masterbate. If you look at the last couple of them, policies or contractors, things that are heavily used, constantly used in an organization. Every time you want to close a deal with the supplier or with a customer, it's very likely that you have a contract and some policies in place. This is what we call a masturbator, and this is by nature, again, non-transactional. Well, we have another bit of master data, which is reference state reference to dark static identifiers.

You can also describe them as in a standardized list of values, reference database units of measurement, kg lbs. Country codes or countries. France, the U.S., India, Canada. These are static lists of values, corporate codes, weight, temperature length, calendars, dates. This is reference data. This rarely changes. And they are usually a start. The objects are very similar across multiple companies, whereas master data can differ based on the products that the company sells or the services already or the activity that they have. Let's see how. Why must the data be important and how some success stories translated master data into business. The AMAA, the Alberta Motor Association, is an advocate for tracked traffic strata safety in Canada.

The customer data was being captured across multiple business lines. I'd like memberships, travel, insurance. There are many ways for you to become an MBA customer. An MBA then implemented an MBM solution to consolidate all this customer information. And let's see what happened. From twelve millions total customer records collected from here and there. Duplicate. It's the same person in two different systems and all these kinds of things. Remember data quality and application synchronization across systems. So with this data quality exercise using master data, they went down to three million customers. So imagine the difference of, for example, contacting twelve million users versus contacting three million users.

And how then you can do segmentation and have a customer record that is a real customer and needs the same customer across all platforms. Customer golden records and customer database consolidation has become a political map of many companies and so many businesses are implementing data management systems to make sure that they are talking only to one customer. Another example is our product risks Vista. It's an outdoor manufacturer that manufactures goods for outdoor living and outdoor activities, and they found that the data was very easy to go rogue.

May is going rogue, that they might have some processes or ways of creating data that will create silos or data will be isolated in one place. And it's not talking to the rest of the enterprise systems. What they did is they implemented an MDMA solution for 60000 products, including retirement workflows. The result of this was 30 million dollars identified in products as addresses. What does it mean to address products that were forgotten on the shelf, products that were going out of season? Product didn't have a time and workflows because their products are replaced by new versions of the same. And all these products were where we're stocking up on the shelves. And they identified up to 30 million of these products.

Another example, how masturbators can consolidate the frequent information used in a corporation or any in a company like are the products that they manufacture. A summary of massive data is that it refers to the most important data that is owned by a company. It can be their products. It can be the list of services. It can be their contracts. It can be the rates. But this is the most important data that a company must have.

It has common definitions across an organization as reference data. It's an external memory, for example, countries or dates and usually are startling. Mustardy is a voracious asset for companies. It's the bread and butter of any business. And it's important to be organized and accessible in the next chapter. They get

# Data Privacy

How are companies and governments using your data? Are their movements being tracked? How did that company get your phone number? Can you read my account and all my data? All these questions have become natural for many of us today. We will talk about data rights, information, and privacy. Is the relationship between the collection and dissemination of data. It is also known as data privacy or data protection. Why is data privacy important? Number one, because data is one of the most important assets.

A company has a breach at the corporation and we have seen it already. Few in the last year can put proprietary data in the hands of a competitor or can leak information about a lot of consumers or their credit cards. Privacy is the right of an individual to be free from uninvited surveillance. What that means is that you have your right to say that you don't want to be tracked or that you're the one with your data to be shared with other companies or with other people. It applies to me. It spans across all data analytics, works descriptive, predictive and prescriptive and disciplines. It applies to the data that is stored either in the data warehouse or in any data set.

Some of the tools used for data privacy are data grail won trust and big I.T. and best practices are minimal data collection. Just collect the data that you need. Data ownership and encryption. How this data privacy looks around the world. This mob from Dealy Piper data protection shows an enigma. In a glimpse what's the current status? You can see that North America and

Europe and some parts of Asia and Southeast Asia are quite heavy in regulation and enforcement. Enforcement of the data, privacy of the ownership of data of their consumers, people, users. Whereas all parts of the world are a bit more light.

Let's look in detail at some regions to see how this is enforced and how this looks like the GDP area requires all data controllers and data processors that handle personal data to apply appropriate security and organizational measures in order to safeguard the confidentiality, integrity and availability of processing services. GDP, RDA European Regulation for Data Privacy. It was enacted in 2016 but came only enforceable on May 25th of 2018. It started being valid from 2018. Since then, there have been a few warnings, but also a few fines and which stressed how important data privacy has become in the European Union in 2020. This year, in January, after receiving hundreds of complaints from customers receiving unsolicited commercial communications made without constant T. I am an Italian telecommunications company operator and was fined twenty eight million euros. This is not the biggest find that the European Union has had, but I think the biggest.

It's British Airways with 200 million euros. But this is not yet final. The highest fine has been applied to Google for not ensuring proper handling of the data. With 50 million euros, let's have a look at the US. The US has data privacy laws, but there isn't a central federal level privacy law like the GDP that applies in Europe. There are several vertically focused federal privacy laws, like four different verticals. There are different laws that apply for data acquisition, storage and usage. And there are other laws at the state level that defend the consumers and their data. But as such, the message is that the US doesn't have so far federal country wise privacy law in China. And in March 2013, they issued a national standard, which is that I was following the principles of their GDP.

They cover the collection and storage and use of data and disclosure of personal information. South Korea last year, in 2019, enforced a new privacy law that has several points that must be accepted for every customer to use the data at each level. So this is adding a new level of granularity and complexity to the data privacy in South Korea. Companies must explain the disclosure and what data they are collecting and why they want to do it. It must be stated upfront. They must allow you to opt out and stop collecting data if you don't want to. They need to inform you if your data is going to be shared with third parties, with other companies. If the data is transferred outside the contract, the country, they must inform the consumer, the customer, the owner of the data, but also the local institutions.

Every time you ask for it, you are allowed to receive a copy of all your data. What a company has is stored and in terms of your personal data and the companies are also required to maintain accurate records. In summary, data privacy is a right to take control of the data that you share. Companies need to be respectful and transparent with the data of their customers or employees. Last, data privacy will evolve with technology as there is an ethical debate linked to data and analytics. How much data should we be using? Put analytics. The ethical debate is open and it's here to stay.

How much can companies say that less behavior is strictly personal as a source? Every company and governments need to ensure that data is carefully handled. It follows the privacy premise established by each country. Your data is your life and it's yours. We are praying for the end of the mining of data management. The problem is chapters will learn about the data lifecycle too.